IMAGINE
THROUGH THE EYES OF...

CREATIVE STARS

Edited By Jenni Harrison

First published in Great Britain in 2023 by:

Young Writers® Est. 1991

Young Writers
Remus House
Coltsfoot Drive
Peterborough
PE2 9BF
Telephone: 01733 890066
Website: www.youngwriters.co.uk

All Rights Reserved
Book Design by Davina Hopping
© Copyright Contributors 2022
Softback ISBN 978-1-80459-288-5

Printed and bound in the UK by BookPrintingUK
Website: www.bookprintinguk.com
YB0528I

FOREWORD

WELCOME READER,

For Young Writers' latest competition Imagine, we asked primary school pupils to look beyond themselves, to think about the lives and inner thoughts of others and to put themselves in their shoes, and then write a poem about it!

Here at Young Writers our aim is to encourage creativity in children and to inspire a love of the written word, so it's great to get such an amazing response, with some absolutely fantastic poems. It's important for children to focus on and celebrate others and this competition allowed them to explore and develop their empathy, taking the time to consider the emotions and experiences of others. Whether that was their favourite celebrity, a fictional character or even their pet hamster, they rose to the challenge magnificently! The result is a collection of thoughtful and moving poems in a variety of poetic styles that also showcase their creativity and writing ability.

I'd like to congratulate all the young poets in this anthology, it's a wonderful achievement and I hope this inspires them to continue with their creative writing.

CONTENTS

Independent Entries

Nazifa Rehman (9)	1
Mehreen Azim (10)	2
Lara Brooks (10)	6
Lucas Jackson (10)	8
Claudia Castley (10)	10
Huzaifa Hassan (10)	12
Demi-Maria Panchal (8)	14
Millie Pearson (9)	16
Crystal-Marie Davenport (5)	18
Matilda Cooper (10)	20
Atisha Patel (11)	22
Angelika Afanasyeva	24
Livvi Gradwell (10)	26
Arlo O'Sullivan (8)	28
Arnav Patil (10)	30
Aliza Khan (9)	31
Bonnie McGlashan (11)	32
Scarlett Hay (9)	34
Indigo Jones	35
Esther Akinwonmi-Pedro (8)	36
Ayesha Mohammed (9)	37
William Llewelyn Jones (9)	38
Ata Khalaf (10)	39
Nafisa Arafat (10)	40
Aneel Kaur Kooner (9)	41
Luke Withers (10)	42
Nina Zych-Twaddell (10)	43
Kohinoorjot Kaur (9)	44
Dillon O'Rourke (9)	45
Defne Degirmenci (9)	46
Freya Enfield (10)	47
Shiza Jahangir (10)	48
Ganisha Jeyathas (10)	50
Osaremen Atoe (10)	51
Anabia Eman (12)	52
Chloe Griffiths (11)	53
Sarah Shaikh (10)	54
Kabiven Vivekanantharajah (10)	55
Luqman Ahmad (9)	56
Callum Wong (9)	57
Evie Rudolph (10)	58
Shiyam Thulasiraj	59
Liberty McKenzie (10)	60
Reuben Pushpananthan (10)	61
Meerab Fatima (11)	62
Oliver Tan (7)	63
Devna Sanal (8)	64
Sky Kwok (8)	65
Yuveer Goenka (8)	66
Ayana Ahmed (8)	67
Eshaal Naeem (6)	68
Brook Laycock (9)	69
Maša Koronić (7)	70
Arnan Taylor (6)	71
Isabelle Freya George (10)	72
Imaani Hussain (8)	73
Umaymah Hussain (9)	74
Nva Kawa (8)	75
Fabian Popa (7)	76
Jessica Wang (9)	77
Sophie Marsh (5)	78
Serena Esme Dhillon (9)	79
Aiza Ali (7)	80
Isabella McEwan (10)	81
Fouzia Ouddah (10)	82
Zain Rehman (5)	83
Leo Wong (6)	84
Vasanthi Siddula	85
Olivia Marsh (8)	86

Omar Faisal (7)	87
Javeria Safdar Chaudhary	88
Mohammad Ubaidullah (7)	89
Anjali Ramalingam (7)	90
Frankie Halford (9)	91
Noah Ryan Massey (6)	92
Jules Berthet (10)	93
Amir Gyunduz (10)	94

St Cuthbert's RC Primary School, Cardiff Bay

Linah Elhag (10)	95
Sara Orozgani	96
Martha Devereux (9)	98
Leo John Tylke (9)	100
Blake Parris	101
God'sthrone Davids (9)	102
Isis Urzedo Zucolli	103
Amara Elgabar (10)	104
Nailah Ellis (10)	105
Inayah Carpin (10)	106
Genelia Sharif (10)	107
Falak Navabjan	108
Anas Albalawi	109
Rayanna Abyan	110
Suhaib Hassan (10)	111

St George's Primary School, Church Gresley

Ellie Grainger (10)	112
Reuben Marshall (10)	113
Ethan Colley (10)	114
Abigail Hawksworth (10)	115
Charlotte Roden (10)	116
Harrison Poulton (10)	117
Isla Wilson (10)	118
William Hadley (10)	119
Ava Mcclenahan (11)	120
Harry Topliss (10)	121
Orla-Lily Edwards (10)	122
Zack Gee (10)	123
Amarla-Rose Armstrong (10)	124

Ben Sparshott (10)	125
Kayden Murdoch (11)	126
Jonah Hallam (10)	127
Joe Haywood (10)	128
Phoebe Rand (10)	129
Alfie Haywood (10)	130
Riley Ross (10)	131
Niamh Flynn (10)	132
Olivia Evans (11)	133

St Joseph's Catholic Primary School, Northfleet

Leonida-Lilly Saez Mortimer (9)	134
Flavia Mazzocca (8)	135
Freddy Lawlor (8)	136
Temilayo Adesina (8)	137
Michael Ayenuro (10)	138
Alya Shah (8)	139
Ite Jolaoso (10)	140
Connie Oxtoby (8)	141
Enyinna Okolie (8)	142
Kyra Manan (9)	143
Hannah Mahon (10)	144

Stroud Green Primary School, London

Aaliyah Oluseye (10)	145
Nate Gosling (10)	146
Nilay Dogruoglu (11)	147
Fernando Goncalves Miguel (10)	148
Mouna Ahouddar (10)	149
Alessandro Boghean (10)	150
Zinedine Laifa (10)	151
Suzie Parker (10)	152
Darla Thomas-Thompson (10)	153
Laurence Lachmann (10)	154
Xianna Rose-Locke (8)	155
Yanaëlle B (8)	156
Iris Mcananey (8)	157
Hayaat Mohamed (10)	158
Rosa Niland (10)	159
Miska Barton (10)	160

Zoe Katona (10) 161

The Sir Donald Bailey Academy, Newark

Chloe Parker (10)	162
Amelia Needham (10)	163
Isabella Hudson (10)	164
Ashley Muller (10)	166
Paige Keetley (10)	167

Wold Newton Foundation School, Wold Newton

Amelie Scott (10)	168
Georgia Emmerson (10)	170
Joseph Newton (11)	172
Ebony Warters (10)	174
Ellie Davison (11)	176
Rose Harrison (10)	178
Dallas Kirman (9)	180
Lorence Blyth (10)	181
Laycie Rutherford (11)	182
Emma-Jo Wheeler (9)	184
Lily Yeadon (10)	186
Emily Garrick	187
Toby Pinder (11)	188
Charlie Emmerson (9)	190
William Traves (10)	191
Lewis Kirk (10)	192
Lailah Chandler (10)	193

THE POEMS

It's Me, Earth!

I'm rotating around the sun 24 hours a day,
I'm watching all the countries, observing kids as they play,
We're ninety-three million miles away,
All of our countries having fun in their own ways,
Japanese, Hindi, Farsi, Arabic, Italian, Moroccan,
A hundred languages being spoken everywhere all day.

So many abilities and human rights there are inside me,
But let's not forget about animals as they spread kindness around me,
Cows make milk, cheese and yoghurt and hens lay eggs for us to eat,
So many jobs whirl around me such as doctors, police, nurses, and scientists.

Now you can imagine how I am,
I'm a mind-whirling planet filled with emotions and brisk,
Having to do so much work all day,
Workaholic parents are on their way!

Nazifa Rehman (9)

My Winters

The winters are cold,
The winters are bold,
They are harsh and colder than the coldest marsh,
But here I am on the streets,
Just looking at people's treats,
The worst place to be is me,
My name is May and I was born on a day,
When the snow covered the ground,
And people barely made a sound,

I am telling you about my winter,
Today is so frigid I feel like I am rigid,
There are frozen lakes and rivers,
The winds also give me shivers,
I live in a hut,
All it has is an old table which is very stable,
Plus a rattan stool from the native hut,
And a chair made of heavenly coconut,
I sleep on the floor,
'Cause I'm very poor,
I don't even have a door,

I would love to huddle around a fire,
And pull my shutters tight,
But the snow only piles higher and higher,
And the world around me turns white,
I have nothing to aspire,

I have nothing to admire,
My brain feels as if it's on fire,
But now I am on my way,
Because today is a very special day,
The rich folks sit at a table,
And they are loaded down with fancy fare,
And they dressed in awesome satin and sable,
And their eyes are blinded by their gold silverware,

I can collect all the leftover stuff,
But my journey is not yet over it is still rough,
On my way, I met a lady who looked very kind,
For me, that is a person which is very hard to find,
She took me into her cosy home,
And brushed my hair with a comb,

I called her Mrs,
And she showered me with kisses,

She gave me some food,
It was so yummy it had such a taste,
It certainly did not deserve to go to waste,
The lady told me to go to a red cosy bed,
With a promise of a breakfast of good old bread,
I woke up at the break of dawn,
And let out an almighty yawn,
I went downstairs and sat at the table which surprisingly was very sturdy and stable,
She gave me a meal it was such a meal,

It seemed really really unreal,
She told me as I started to play that I would make a journey this very day,
You make a journey far and far away,
On a path, no human has ever dared to stray,
And on the way, you will have no time to play no place to stay,
She brushed my hair and gave me a glare,
And told me to pack up right now somehow,
I've come back from the journey ages ago,
The lady who told me to go on the journey that very day,

Her name was Kay,
That was ages ago and now I am fine,
I came back when I was still in my prime,
Now I am rich I'm lucky Kay wasn't a witch,
She was my mother all along,
I love her with my heart nothing
can break us apart.

Mehreen Azim (10)

Please Recycle Me!

Left to rot, I don't think so!
I don't biodegrade, didn't you know?
I wrap and I twist,
But being left on the ground, that's not the gist.
Biodegrading sounds like fun,
But I am stuck lying around with everyone.

When am I going to succumb?
I know from personal experience, in fact, it is glum!
I can't rot,
And left in this spot
I get blown around with the leaves
Won't someone just rescue me, please?

Not in the bin with all that litter,
No, I'd rather be left to flitter.
Can't you see my little sign?
Three green arrows spinning around,
Oh please, don't just leave me on the ground.

Here I am left to rot,
Whenever people see me, they are off like a shot.

They say, "Eew, look at that junk left on the ground!
Shouldn't it be in the dump?"
No, why can't they see?
Look - you can recycle me!

A girl walked past with a litter picker
Oh, I better fly quicker
But when I was grasped
She did not put me in the bin but simply asked
"You're recyclable, aren't you?"
So now I'm in a factory and being reused.
Now guess what I am?
I'll leave that to you.

Lara Brooks (10)

Autism

Thunder and lightning strike me again,
Making the thundering bulldozers in my eardrums get going that I contain.
Whether it's people shouting, vehicles rumbling or anything else ear-piercing, the bulldozers attack.
Roses are red, violets are blue,
But what colour is autism? I have not a clue.
Take me, books, take me away to somewhere where it is silent,
So I can be free on this treasure island.
No smells of disgusting food, or any weird artefacts that have the texture of strange.
Just peaceful and relaxing with nothing to bother me.
But no! This is Earth, a planet that does nothing but put pressure on you.
When you go to the door, the planet has taken away your other shoe.
When you go to collect something that someone has told you to collect, it turns out that it's not even there.
Why is the world targeting me? I haven't done anything wrong, have I?

All I do is show off my talent for drawing and writing, that wouldn't even hurt an eye.
For some reason, when I have a hug or take a break with a stretchy man, the world likes me again.
Why is this? I will never know,
World, when you do take a break, don't say I didn't tell you so.

Lucas Jackson (10)

Splish, Splash, Splosh!

Splish, splash, splosh!

The raindrops fall on my face
Splish, splash, splosh!
I giggle and I imagine I was a raindrop up there.

I would feel the cool wind.
Swish, swish, swish!
I would be in a big cloud
Which would be fun and loud.

I would drop from the sky
Splish, splash, splash!
I would land on wet, soft green ground
Without making much sound.

I would see the old oak tree swaying in the wind
Swish, swish, swish!
What a beautiful sight,
An old tree with such a height

I would see lots of animals like hedgehogs, foxes and birds
Chirp, chirp, chirp!

I would hear the gurgle of the stream
And I would feel happy and beam

I would see wonderful leaves on the ground and on the trees
Swish, swash, swish!
I would roll around with fun
Waiting for the sun.

Then I would feel the warm rays of the sun
Warm, warm, warm!
The sun would shine bright
And I would evaporate again out of sight.

With the water cycle
I would travel to the clouds again
Swish, swosh, swish!
How wonderful it would be
To be a little raindrop like me.

Claudia Castley (10)

Clamber And Slumber Mountain Dream

Finally, the amazing day is here,
Going to ascend a magnificent mountain,
Backpack ready with all equipment,
Morale so high,
And say goodbye.

I'm at base camp ready to go,
Summit high up in the sky,
Hard to climb but I'll try,
Harness tight and on my way,
Slippery snowy mountain let me stay.

Suddenly! My harness gets loose,
I'm frightened, I'm scared,
What do I do?
Maybe I'll fall.

I scratched and kicked the rugged rock,
Trying to hold it tight,
Losing hope and sigh!

A supportive hand at my back,
Pushes me up the precipice,
At last, back on the hard, grey jagged rock,
Shivering and trembling with fear

Approached the beautiful, white, snowcapped peak,
Whoo hoo!
I conquered the summit at last.

The magnificent view,
My tired frosty eyes filled with happiness,
Glad to be on the abseil mountain,
Looking down at the base and I think
It is me who clambered and made my dream come true!

Huzaifa Hassan (10)

The River

The River's a vagrant,
A cloud, a vagabond,
She is always busy, a busy, busy bee,
She will never stop to be just like a pond.

The River's a wispy strand of hair,
Through villages and mountains,
A sapphire-blue ink trail,
At the start and bottom of fountains.

The River's a copy of Fagin,
She hides them away,
The casket of shining riches,
That never in her eyes could grow grey.

The River's a delicate seed,
She is humming and she is giggling,
Glamorous, ravishing and shining,
And on a sunny day, always relaxing.

The River's a mischievous mime,
She leaps and she darts,

Gushing, flowing, storming through forests,
She never gives a break to her heart.

The River's a kitten, an angel, a pug, a cute and cuddly teddy bear,
A harmonious, gentle bunny,
It's sparkly gold, luminous aqua-blue, how lovely!
The elegant fish, you may think funny!

Demi-Maria Panchal (8)

I'm A Plastic Bottle

I'm a plastic bottle, as happy as could be,
Sitting on the shelf thinking of an amazing life ahead of me,
One day somebody opened the fridge door,
It was my time to shine and sitting on the shelf was no more.
My hopes were high as we left the shop
Thinking about all my hopes and dreams
As my bottle top went pop!
But soon my dreams were dashed
As my contents were guzzled
And I was thrown on the floor as trash.
See I'm not just a plastic bottle,
I have many hidden uses.
I could have been a pencil case
Sitting on the children's desk seeing the smiles spread across their face
I could have been the parts of many many cars
Driving through the streets at night seeing the many beautiful stars.
Or maybe I could have been a bird feeder, filled up with food to keep the birds alive.

See I'm a piece of plastic, there are so many things I could be,
If only somebody could have recycled me!

Millie Pearson (9)

Mummy

I miss my mummy every day.
When I have nightmares only my big sister comes to my aid.
Me and my big sister are living with other people and not my mummy.

When we see our mummy I play my guitar
And sing a song for my mummy
Saying "I love you, Mummy, yes I do,
I love you lots, lots and lots,
You're my mummy and I miss you lots."
And my sister will be playing on her phone.

My mummy spoils me and my sister once a month,
As that's when she gets to see us
Which is not fair as we want to see her every day.
I miss sitting on my bed with my mummy
Watching Finley the fire engine.
Then when I fall asleep she turns my TV off
And puts my night light on,
She goes to sit with my big sister in her room till she falls asleep.

When we had nightmares we always got in my mummy's big bed.
Snuggled up altogether. I miss that.

Crystal-Marie Davenport (5)

Red Panda Mischief

Crunch,
I munch,
Eating the ants one by one,
One baby ant cries,
"Hold on, hold on!"
I stare at it,
I have no mercy,
The ant cries,
"Please don't hurt me!
Spare us, spare my family,
We've done no wrong, we just want to be free!"
I open my mouth and bare my fangs,
But in actual fact, I had a plan,
"I'm sorry," I said,
I never knew,
That little creatures had feelings too,
Little ant please do you know
The best spot to go,
To find juicy leaves,
Please.

The little ant smiled at me and said,
"The best place to go is little leaf shed,
It's a human's garden,
But the human is kind she even fed,
My whole entire family,"
So off I strolled happy as can be,
Found Little Leaf shed,
And I could see,
That it was the best place for a red panda to be.

Matilda Cooper (10)

The Earth's Wishes

I am a special planet you see,
Full of all living things and glee.
I am full of water, air and life,
But also rife.

You use my land, air, water and soil,
But contain it with litter and rubbish allowing it to spoil.
I give you all of your heads,
Yet you ask for more than I can feed.
With greedy lust, you destroy the nature I give,
How can I properly live?

You pollute my air with smoke, that makes my breath choke
Because you cut down my green forests
And pushed up the greenhouse gases.
I had a clean sea and pure soil,
It is now barren, clogged up with waste and greasy oil.

I have given your life
And you almost put me to my death.

I give you all I have unto my end:
Now, will you cope and finally defend?

Atisha Patel (11)

Dancing Alone

The story begins,
With a ghostly smile,
Still lingering on the face,
Like a bitter aftertaste.

The cheery lad,
Incapable of making anyone sad,
My dancing teacher,
The one that taught me how to bend,
How to make a short, graceful descend,
Opening new moves like a friend,
And teaching me ballet,
Until god marched him to the valley,
Of sorrow.

I copied the moves till I got sore,
He would slowly explain,
Talking when he was sane,
Alive.

The time I took the eerie stage,
I was so used to him being on the same page,

Standing by me,
Twirling by me.

I didn't feel like dancing,
Ever again,
The torture of losing him, the pain,
Was what seemed to turn me insane.

I arched my back the last time,
I twirled better than I have ever done,
My hands twirled,
Like doves in the sky,
As I danced my silent goodbye.

Angelika Afanasyeva

The Cat's Morning

The feel of grass brushing my paw
The soothing scent as the morning dew rises from the floor
The gentle breeze brushing my ear
The trees rustling is all I can hear

The occasional tweet from birds up high
I watch them as they soar through the sky
The blazing sun starting to rise
I stare at it with great, round eyes

Small bright bursts of yellow dot the grass
They gleam in the sun as I pass
Papery orange leaves flutter from their branches
They float down doing their dances

The slightest, tiniest noise captures me
Could it be the thing of my dream
Where, at the mention of it, I beam
The sweet aroma dances through my nose
I search around for where the smell rose
As silent and stealthy as possible
I feel unstoppable

There it is
Basking in the sun's bliss
I get ready to pounce
On this delicious mouse.

Livvi Gradwell (10)

Food And Drink

Chicken nuggets are my favourite,
Especially with chips.
With a side of watermelon of course,
But without the dark, slippery pips.

I love eating doughnuts,
Especially with the crunchy icing.
The sprinkles always get stuck in my teeth,
And the jam doughnuts are the most enticing.

Pez sweets are really fizzy,
And crunchy in my mouth.
They whizz across the room, out of the toy,
And fly around the house.

Coca-Cola is really bubbly,
When I pour it into my mug.
It fizzes and bubbles in my tummy,
Like a small, irritating bug.

I prefer my steak to be medium,
But sometimes I will have it rare.

With curly fries and ketchup of course,
But certainly no hair!

Food and drink are my favourite things to have,
Especially after school.
I can relax and enjoy the yummy taste,
And sometimes I even drool.

Arlo O'Sullivan (8)

The River Of Rubbish

"What happened?" I asked the river,
"Why are you so bitter?"
"Please help me," said the river,
"I'm full of litter."

"What's wrong?" I asked the river,
"I can't see your sand."
"Help me," said the river,
"By giving me a helping hand."

"Why don't you pout?" I asked the river,
"Why don't you stop?"
"I'll tell you why I don't stop," said the river,
"Because I have more rubbish than a corner shop."

"Oh, river!" I sighed,
"Is that a tear?"
"Yes, it is," the river sobbed,
"Humans never changing is my biggest fear."

Arnav Patil (10)

The Earth Speaks

The turning Earth both in a sombre voice,
"Four seasons I give you," its deep voice said
"I give you spring when the lilacs bloom
I give you autumn when the maple is red!

Summer, I give you all crowned with sunshine
And winter of snow and icicle spears.
Four seasons I give you with all their joys
And all the pleasures and all their fears!

Take my four gifts and use each one
Use each wisely, kindly and well
So that record you date to tell."

The turning Earth spoke but once again
"Four seasons I give you," its voice was low
"The gifts are yours and yours is the task
To use my gifts as best you know."

Aliza Khan (9)

Through A Panda's Eyes

I used to be safe and happy
But now I have a different story,
I was enjoying life eating bamboo
But now I am feeling blue
My habitat is getting torn down
I have nowhere to go,
No place to call home,
I am no longer free,
I have nowhere to be,
I got put in a crate
Put on a boat for freight
I thought I was going somewhere safe,
Instead, I was going across the world,
I got put in a dusty, dirty, dilapidated cage,
I was full of rage,
All day long people came to see me,
But I still wasn't happy,
Until one day a lady came along,
And broke me out,
It was a normal night
But I heard a noise that gave me a fright,

I then realised they were here to save me,
They got me out and took me back home,
I got back to my normal life
And I wasn't sad!

Bonnie McGlashan (11)

A Walk In The Woods

My mind is racing, where are we going?
There aren't any familiar noises
We have stopped
I am incredibly curious about what this spectacular scent is
I am filled with anticipation and excitement for the next hill
Why does everything smell so yummy?
Ooh, ooh! Another dog! Got to say hi
"Woof, woof!"
This stick smells and looks like a treat
We have started to speed up now, there is a lot of water falling from the sky
I am okay though, I could walk forever
We have turned around, I don't know why, I was enjoying myself
We have arrived back at the car, but I don't want to go
Ooh, ooh, they have treats!

Can't wait for my next walk!

Scarlett Hay (9)

Earth Is Dying

I am Earth and I am disappointed,
It always hurts to find my rivers polluted,
My air is filled with poisonous gas,
I hate seeing my animals being killed and eaten,
It honestly feels like I, Mother Earth, have been beaten,
Nature and plants are being squashed by rubble,
Wow, I really am in trouble,
I hate seeing animals being chucked into a cage,
You see? We really aren't on the same page,
Chopping down trees, I wish that was a myth,
Eating meat and fish?
That's not cool, it's just cruel,
Can't you see? This is immature,
You're killing my wildlife and nature!
This is bad, this is not good,
So spread the word,
Earth is dying.

Indigo Jones

Holiday Park Home

At Clacton-on-Sea, I can see the brilliantly shining sky as the radiantly blue Maldives Sea.
In the wonderful summer at Clacton-on-Sea, it serves as our vacation home.
The air is so clean and the atmosphere is so peaceful that I can smell it.
My little sister and my big brother and I are dancing.
I can hear the waves of the ocean and we clap hands in time to the beat of sea chants.
My parents laugh as they watch us with amusement.
The wind makes the trees sway as the leaves rustle, flap and cling to the branches.
As my stomach growls in want for freshly cooked fish and chips, the aroma overpowers me.
Being in this holiday park home makes my heart pleased, I can feel it.

Esther Akinwonmi-Pedro (8)

Through The Eyes Of A Polar Bear

G rowl goes the polar bear because of
L itter in places it shouldn't be
O il in the ocean and Lego in the sea
B ears, leopards, turtles and pandas too
A re to name just a few endangered animals
L osing their homes and families because of what humans do!

W e can help save our planet if we
A re more self-aware, things like,
R ecycling, reducing and reusing
M ay prove that we care
I cebergs melt while rainforests burn
N ow is the time that we really should learn
G rowl my furry friend, growl as loud as you can!

One day we will hear you and understand.

Ayesha Mohammed (9)

Trees

Some people think trees are bad, but I think trees are very nice.
They give homes to lots of animals, especially the mice!

Sometimes trees are cut down which makes me full of stress,
They sometimes land on animals, which really makes a mess!

Don't worry, people plant trees, which grow to be big and strong,
So sometimes cutting trees down isn't always wrong!

It's called the ecological life cycle, which gives us lots of trees,
Which gives us lots of oxygen which really helps us breathe!

It also gives us energy, which makes us run around,
Or powers lots of racecars, which cover lots of ground!

So help us, please! Help the trees!

William Llewelyn Jones (9)

I'm Scared

I'm only little,
I'm very scared,
Everything is insanely huge.

I've lost my family due to inhumanity,
On my own, so bored, so bored,
Plastic everywhere dangerously lying around in the open,
As a consequence, I have become as isolated as a human being,
Trying to stay away from a serious disease.

Oh, why can't it be like the old times?
Every person, every single person, child or adult was so considerate,
That no one was even carrying tons of plastic around with them.

I'm only little,
I'm very scared,
Please change our precious world.

Ata Khalaf (10)

Land Of Paradise

As your fork scrapes the plate
Your mother says it's way too late
It's time for bed
Is what she says
As my head hits the pillow
I dream away
As I turn into a phoenix and fly away
Where am I? is what I say
As I realise I'm in a land of paradise
Hooray!
Magical creatures wander around
As some are hissing but some will growl
Chocolate rivers, sweets and lollies
You munch and crunch
And gobble away
But then you hear a voice in your brain
"Nafisa, Nafisa wake up
It's time for school!"
But then I realise you're too cool.

Nafisa Arafat (10)

Elephant's Exciting Adventure

I woke up one morning and decided to travel the world,
Nervous but excited, my textured trunk curled.

Pretty as a picture, the sun rose high,
Golden fields stretched for miles; I could cry!

Oh no! Crocodile! Deadly to the touch,
Run, run quick! Don't get in his clutch!

A curious whiff of fish brought me to Fleetwood,
I'd be a seagull sunbathing on the beach if I could.

A cacophony of drums as the band marched by,
London town was here; the Queen was saying goodbye.

Elephant, elephant, I stand tall
My journey's been the best of all.

Aneel Kaur Kooner (9)

Christmas, Why Can't It Be All Year?

Christmas, why can't it be all year?
Christmas reindeer approaching near,

Why can't snowmen stay all year round?
Dancing all night without a sound,

Why can't luminous lights stay out?
Illuminating without doubt,

Why can't trees with arms held out wide?
See the baubles grinning, then hide,

Why can't paper stay a bright cloth?
Stars dancing as little moths,

Why can't tasty turkey stay here?
Succulent sausage meat all year,

Christmas reindeer approaching near,
A happy Christmas and new year.

Luke Withers (10)

I Am A Tree

I am a tree...

When it is spring, I am covered in blossoms,
Pink flowers, white flowers, I look just awesome!

When it is summer, I am covered in fruit,
Just pick some, and don't you think I look cute?

When it is autumn, my leaves go red,
And gold and amber, I guess they're ready for bed.

When it is winter, I am all bare.
Come on, oh come on! It's just not fair!

Then the cold, white snowflakes fall,
Covering me and covering me so I look like a ball.

And then it's spring again, hooray!
This can start all over again, day by day!

Until the two warm seasons end,
And it will be cold again, my friend.

Nina Zych-Twaddell (10)

I Am A Tree

I am a tree,
I stand tall and proud,
I blossom in the sun,
I dance in the wind.

My trunk is as thick as a giant toe,
My leaves blow in the morning breeze,
My branches reach high as the dreamy clouds,
My roots dig deep into the ground.

In the winter I like to wear a snow crown,
In the spring I like to wear a blossom ballgown,
In the summer I like to bathe in the sparkling sunlight,
In the autumn I like to shed my golden leaves.

The years go by as quick as a flash,
The seasons now repeat year by year,
I am now older but wiser.

Kohinoorjot Kaur (9)

Escape To Safety

Imagine if... I had to leave all I loved behind
My house, my street, my bed, my school, my friends,
And travel to another place
Just to make sure I was safe.

Imagine if... instead of rain it was bombs
And instead of hail, it was bullets
Raining down on my street
We were in trouble of defeat.

Imagine if... I lost someone, someone close to me
I would cry and cry till my eyes were cried out
Knowing I would never see them again
I wish that never happened to them.

Imagine if... there was a place to go
A place of safety from the war
No bullets, no bombs, no guns or death
Somewhere I was safe and could do my best.

Dillon O'Rourke (9)

Winter

W indows gleamed brightly like the sun as the dense fog drooped translucently
I cy lace hung over the chilly, frozen city as a solitary snowflake drifted frostily
N ightfall loomed over everything, concealing it with utter darkness
T he veil of mist clung to the starless night sky, unaccompanied
E erie silence lingered while the tall buildings emerged out of nowhere. Abandoned houses longed for a single person to walk in
R estlessly, a little girl crunched through the blanket of thick pure snow, wondering why the streets were so empty.

Defne Degirmenci (9)

We Imagined

I imagine that I will be a professional poem writer.
My friend imagines that she will be a professional horse rider.
We imagined that when we first met, we would be best friends.

I imagine we will be friends no matter what.
My friend imagines the same thing.
We imagined that we would do the same things and like the same things even though we knew it wouldn't work.

I imagined that we will keep in touch
Even though she moved away.
She imagined going to Wales and missing me
We imagined that we would both miss each other.
I imagine a time when I will see my friend again.

Freya Enfield (10)

I'm Earth!

I see smoke
They burn things on me
I see pollution
Now I don't understand.
If I'm filled with smoke then what am I?
I'm Earth!
Say hi!

I see litter,
They throw it on me.
I see plastic,
It fills my seas.
If I'm full of rubbish then what am I?
I'm Earth!
Say hi!

I see heat,
They say global warming.
I see fires and electricity
They burn so much
If I'm so hot then what am I?

I'm Earth!
Say hi!

I see pollution
I see rubbish
I see global warming
I'm so ill and need to recover
If I'm so sick then what am I?
I'm not Earth.
Say goodbye.

Shiza Jahangir (10)

The Tree...

As I loom over the little people
Who look like puppets
Dancing elegantly across the landscape,

All my beautiful creatures shall rest
From the sun's high tide
They shall be safe and comfortable,

My involucral leaves turn to
Different bright colours
Red, gold and yellow,

But however, I help them
Some incurious people avoid me,

They make me feel
Downhearted and depressed
Filling me with tension.

Would you help me?
Is there any solution to this?

Ganisha Jeyathas (10)

The Day Of A Mother

I look at her.
"You're meaner!"
If only she knew
How I grew.
"Get to school!"
"School doesn't rule!"
A slap, I won't do,
So maybe a talking to?
Mum should come.
It would be as if I was in Year One,
Her twenty-one!
No.
I can do this, even if she goes low.
I need to prove myself,
That I can do this all by myself.
I am a mother,
A strong one not like any other.
So come at me, Jane,
'Cause I will make your eyes rain.

Osaremen Atoe (10)

Through The Eyes Of The Wondrous World

I wake up to see radiant exquisite colours staring right at me streaming through my window wide.
They dance and prance and twirl on a merry ride.
Wondrous thoughts fill my head and run around like a speedy roller coaster.
I am the world, I am the Earth where people like to have some fun.
Every time I see my birds flutter and sing in the sky,
Happiness flows inside of me to see their delighted faces.
Sometimes I wished I could see my people fly.
The shine of the stars,
The feeling of love and passion
That can melt time and wars.

Anabia Eman (12)

Dance

I shudder as I stretch my arms out,
The thudding beat makes me quiver,
Everyone is already done, though I am stuck throughout,
There are hisses and boos from the crowds, but I have yet to deliver,

The ribbons of failure lick my face,
Tempting me, wanting me, teasing me,
I try not to give in to the embrace,
I don't understand, why can't I flee?

I howl and cry,
I lift my leg like an ember,
The beast inside me is ready to prey,
I keep dancing on, though I am tense and tender,
I finish with a curtsy as it envelops me.

Chloe Griffiths (11)

Royal Wild

At the break of dawn
As the rose-red sun drifts to the black sky
Lighting its path in its wake
I scamper around the shrubs and trees
In the hot, dry and grassy savannah
On the lookout for prey, predators and poachers.

They are mean and greedy
They terrorise animals for their meat, bones, oil, etc.
I am an ultra-rare and endangered
King cheetah!
But being rare makes poachers hot on my swift heel
I just wish they would stop being so persistent and stop hunting animals
Especially endangered and rare ones.

Sarah Shaikh (10)

Life Of Me

I can see life by looking at nature
I can smell life by smelling acorns
I can touch life by touching the trees
I can feel life by playing in the park

I can explore life by travelling around the world
I can visit life by meeting my family member
I can feel life by having fun
I can have fun with life by going somewhere

I can learn for life by educating myself
I can read for life by learning new words
I can win for life by earning trophies
I can see life by having a good time.

Kabiven Vivekanantharajah (10)

Words

Don't let words bring you down,
Instead, build some new ground.
When you're ready, you should deal with them
By staying strong as its top revenge.
If you let bullies make you bow
It'll do you no good, I vow.

Whatever they say don't blink an eye,
For cruel words only make you cry.
Do not worry, lovely people are there,
For kindness isn't that rare.
To make the world a better place,
Do good deeds no matter what the case.

Luqman Ahmad (9)

Through The Eyes Of A Wolf

I'm a wolf, black and grey,
Who likes to eat brown deer.
During the day I like to play,
At night I like to cheer.

I'm a wolf with sharp grey claws,
I use them to hunt for food.
My paws are used to do chores,
When I am in a good mood.

I'm a wolf living in a cave,
Where bears eat my precious meat.
I go to the warm lake to bathe,
While I get to have a treat.

I'm a wolf with a long tail,
I have fifteen in my pack.
While hunting I leave a trail,
So there's always an attack!

Callum Wong (9)

Planet Earth

Promise you won't forget me
When you find a better place,
Don't just abandon me,
Destroy me, go away.

I know the ice is melting,
I know the sea levels rise,
But you take up some space with your needs,
With sorrow, love and lies.

You need to make a change,
Stop cutting down my trees,
Stop polluting the seas with plastic
Stop poisoning the air with smoke and steam.

Don't take it all for granted,
There is no Planet B,
So stop this all this instant
Please look after me.

Evie Rudolph (10)

Don't Hurt Me

This ancient animal for years,
Nobody knows who he is!
If you look at his adoring eyes
It would make you cry.

He is very rapid at climbing
But the slowest at walking.
As this animal is a herbivore
It only eats plants.

It lives in the wild.
Still it acts like a child.
What animal could it be?

This animal's skin is black and white,
A multicolour charm.
What could it be?
What could it be?

Shiyam Thulasiraj

Eagle

As I swoop through the forest,
I can see luscious green trees blowing in the wind.

As I swoop through the forest,
I can hear the rustling of my prey below.

As I swoop through the forest,
I can feel the trees brushing against my wings before I dive down to grab my prey.

As I swoop through the forest,
I can taste the bitter air as the wind ruffles my feathers.

As I swoop through the forest,
I can smell the fresh water from the lake as I grab my prey.

Liberty McKenzie (10)

The Prison In My Head

My body gathers anger.
Swallowing up my thoughts.
Locked up on a coat hanger.
My feet are full of warts.

Just in front, before my eyes.
The sun begins to rise.
A ball of fire, a yellow prize.
A screeching hiss of lullabies.

Just like the moon misses the sun.
The waves start to run.
They seek for the lost one.
But that now is gone.

Every night something calls to me.
A lighting strike, the buzz of a bee.
A mouthful of green pea.
No, it's the echo in the prison in me.

Reuben Pushpananthan (10)

Who Am I?

I am a human
Living in this world
Trying my best to earn freedom

This is me
From my head to my toe
From my side to side

I look in the mirror
Who knows what I saw
I saw me
Smiling at my own reflection

I am happy for who I am
What would be better than to be alive?

My face, my hair, my eyes and the rest of my body are all part of me
My wisdom, my health, my safety and my well-being are all part of me
We are all special in our own way
And I love all of me.

Meerab Fatima (11)

The Rainforest

Between the Equator a hidden world of wonder awaits.
Beautiful bird of paradise flowers catch a glimmer in the dark forest floor.
Jaguars prowl through the forest haunting their fearful prey.
Not every crevice is safe, Brazilian wandering spiders hunt down the prey biting them to death.
Flying snakes gracefully glide from tree to tree.
Prying eyes of ocelot shine in the dull and dark forest floor like a gem.
What would we do without this paradise?

Oliver Tan (7)

Best Dive Day

When I awake from the sunlight,
I'm ready for the best day of my life.
I am going to dive underwater,
I will go out to sea like an explorer,
Me and my family did it once
And it was lots of fun!
For breakfast, I ate seaweed food,
It was surprisingly good,
When I put on the diving costume,
The things that I packed
And the gadgets were super cool!
There were beautiful things in the ocean
And my brain had a serene time.
Best dive day ever!

Devna Sanal (8)

Fearful Cloud

I'm as fluffy as a white cloud
As soft as cotton candy
As a timid little girl
I am afraid of loud noises and solitude
My friends always stay with me
It makes me feel safe
Sheer cliffs and tough terrains are my favourite places
My excellent sense of hearing and peripheral vision helps me keep away from predators
People like to treat me with apples and carrots
Children usually know me from fables.

Sky Kwok (8)

Halloween

Vampire teeth must devour
Carved pumpkins roar out light
Zombies rise at the midnight hour
Deadly spider takes the bite

Cobwebs capture his nightmare
A witch's wand waves around
Climb on her broom if you dare
Spooky skeletons rise from the ground

Bare trees reach a black night sky
They reach out for you too
Full moon rise, bats fly high
Run fast or get covered in goo!

Yuveer Goenka (8)

Woolly Winter

Hibernating hedgehogs
Sleeping squirrels
Frozen forests
Spectacular snowballs
Woolly winter

Soft sweaters
Special scarves
Cosy Christmas
Delightful dinners
Woolly winter

Bright, bold boots
Starry snowflakes
Slippery skating
Icy icicles
Woolly winter

Choir concert
Statue snowman
Terrible temperature
Wet wellies
Woolly winter.

Ayana Ahmed (8)

The Sky

At night the sky is dark blue
There are shiny stars and the moon
The sky has fluffy clouds in it
In the sky, the sun is lit
There are colourful rainbows in the sky
There is rain which comes from clouds which are high
There are birds in the sky which fly aeroplanes
Take you to different countries which are nice
There are storms in the sky which cause lightning
Oh, I love the sunset in the sky.

Eshaal Naeem (6)

I'm A Grey Squirrel

I'm a grey squirrel that lives in a tree.
Happy as can be.

Then one day everything changed.
How can that be?

The builders came.
They didn't care about me.

Every day loads of trees
Kept coming down around me.

It was no use
I had lost my home.

Off I went to roam
So I could find another home.

Eventually, I found another tree
I was as happy as can be.

Brook Laycock (9)

Imagine

Imagine our planet without litter,
Imagine it full of flowers and glitter.
Imagine how happy Earth would be,
Imagine it clean and sparkly.
Animals all around running free,
Imagine how wonderful this would be.
Children with smiles on their faces,
Playing hide-and-seek in this place.
That's why you should take care of our planet,
And plant a flower,
We all have that power.

Maša Koronić (7)

What Am I?

I am nocturnal,
I come out at night.
My predator is a badger,
It gives me a fright.
I eat snails, beetles and bugs.
My poo is like a black slug.
I grunt like a pig,
I squeal and snuffle.
In orange and brown crunchy leaves I snuffle.
I am prickly,
I have 5,000 spikes!
I hide in a ball.
I am small and shy.
What am I?

Answer: I am a hedgehog.

Arnan Taylor (6)

Shining Waters

When the sun shines on my silky surface
And the brisk wind blows
My wonderful ripples slowly explode
It used to be a haven but now I'm not so sure
There are monsters at the door
They're bobbing up and down and ruining what was perfect before
The animals in my protection feel
Unsafe and insecure
I'm desperate to help them and to restore it as before
Will someone please help me
Please save my wonderful shore.

Isabelle Freya George (10)

Summertime

I am summertime,
To make me whip up some fluffy clouds.
Mix with two spoonfuls of blue sky,
Add one dollop of yellow sun and a gentle cooling breeze.
Sprinkle in laughing cousins,
Add late-night sleepovers.
Stir in one Nanu growing hot, fiery chillies,
Add in a snoring, sleeping Nana.
Dust over with multicoloured hanging baskets,
Fresh, green parks and scorching sandpits.
Bake with happiness and enjoy…
Me!

Imaani Hussain (8)

Butterfly

Butterfly, butterfly
Go and enjoy your life
Turn towards the blue sky
And fly up ten feet high

Large wings
Beautiful designs
Remember you're divine
When flying up to the sky

One day when you leave this world
Remember your journey to the bright blue sky
Remember the things you did to fly
And the days and days you grew till the very end.

Umaymah Hussain (9)

The Beach

I can see the gorgeous umbrellas
I can see the skilled surfers
I can hear the loud waves
I can hear the seagulls
I can smell suncream
I can smell lemonade
I can feel the powdery sand
I can feel the relaxed atmosphere
I can taste the salty ocean water
I can taste the refreshing ice water
I can feel the pain of the jellyfish sting
I can feel the pain of the burning sun.

Nva Kawa (8)

The Policeman's Life

I am a policeman, strong and healthy,
And my life is a danger.
I save people's lives and I do what I like.
I live at a police station,
Surrounded by sirens on top of our cars.
We have three colours on our cars,
White, blue and yellow,
When people hear our sirens they move out of the way,
This is me.
I am a policeman.

Fabian Popa (7)

Just An Octopus?

We just think
That octopuses live in the sea.
But they're better than that,
Just you wait and see.
They can do anything.
Just give them a chance.
They could dance.
They could fight.
They could even prance.
So, when you see octopuses,
Don't shrug a lot,
And just walk by,
Wait and see,
The glorious thing
Just might make pie.

Jessica Wang (9)

Wasp

I am a wasp
I like to see the birds fluttering in the air
I like flowers and I like the birds twittering in the sky
I like to zigzag in the blue, that's how I like it
And that's how it will stay
I don't like stinging people,
Because I like to be up in the air, ready to spin.

Sophie Marsh (5)

Litter Life

I'm a litter piece
And I live in Greece
I'm next to a bin
And by my side, there's a baked bean tin
Oh how I loved it when I was used
But now I'm a piece of paper bruised
Why am I not important anymore?
It feels like I'm always gonna be stuck here on the floor!

Serena Esme Dhillon (9)

Keep Our Planet Clean

When sailing on a boat
I look at the sea
What do I see?
All I see is litter
What can you see?
What can I do?
Can you help me?
Should I carry on?
Or should I not?
It keeps on spreading
For miles and as far as the eye can see
Oh no,
We can't just watch the sea
We must do all we can to clean the sea.

Aiza Ali (7)

Birds

Flying, swooping above the land
Frightened by loud noises like a band

Watching and hiding from predators below
Building nests for family as soft as a pillow

Finding, searching for food on the ground
I even chirp and sing, but sometimes don't make a sound.

Isabella McEwan (10)

My Teddy, Spain

Imagine being my teddy, Spain,
Always cheering me up when I'm down,
Never leaving me out,
Always making my pain go away.

Making me feel so happy and joyous,
Helping me with my homework,
Playing football with me,
After all, no one can replace my teddy.

Fouzia Ouddah (10)

Seed To Tree

I was small but full of magic
The farmer put me in the soil to see the magic
He gave me water and sunshine to grow
Then I turned into a fruitful tree
I gave you food to keep you healthy
And provided shade to rest underneath me
I was a seed turned into a tree.

Zain Rehman (5)

Little Chicken

I'm a yellow chicken,
Please don't put me in the kitchen.
I don't want to be cooked in the oven,
And be burnt and eaten like my cousin.

I am slow and weak,
I also have a small beak.
Try and catch me if you can,
Run and hide will be my plan.

Leo Wong (6)

My Last Moments

Seventy years of reign
Through happiness and pain
I have served my country
My family lay weeping beside me
In my last moments, I let myself fall
And recollect all my memories
I take Philip's hand and glide away
Ready to start a new adventure.

Vasanthi Siddula

I Don't Belong In The Mediterranean Sea

I am a plain Walkers crisp packet,
Glinting in the hot blazing sun
I am floating in the sea in Majorca
I am heading to Ibiza.

Fierce waves crash on me
I am drowning,
I plummet past stingrays and octopuses
I don't belong in the sea.

Olivia Marsh (8)

I Am A Cat

I am a cat that sits on a mat
I am a cat that chases a rat
I am a cat that hates bats
I am a cat that loves a pat
I am a cat that wears a hat
I am a cat that likes to chat
Meow, meow, meow!

Omar Faisal (7)

Imagine

Imagine freedom
Imagine no wars
Imagine no fights
Imagine peace and harmony
All around the world
Imagine love for everybody
Imagine giving happiness to those who are in pain and in need.

Javeria Safdar Chaudhary

The Hairy Beast

On a deep, dark night
Holding my nerves tight
Deep in the jungle
When I stumble
I saw a hairy beast
Having his feast
I woke up screaming
Realising I was dreaming.

Mohammad Ubaidullah (7)

The Rainbow

I like rainbows.
I wish to see one.
I got outside and lay down in the garden.
I closed my eyes and it appeared -
There was a rainbow!

Anjali Ramalingam (7)

Through The Eyes Of A Rock Climber
A tanka

As I climb on rocks
I use my strength and my tools
I grapple hook up
When I'm climbing I grip on
Without warning the rope slips!

Frankie Halford (9)

Superbunny Go

I am Superbunny
I have a coat of snow
I can pounce down low
When I think about where wild berries grow
Twitchy nose
Wiry whiskers
Look at me go.

Noah Ryan Massey (6)

Polka

A haiku

Cat's fur keeps cats hot
Their fur is grey, black and brown
Sleeping and active.

Jules Berthet (10)

Be The Change!
A haiku

Nature is gorgeous
Earth is no threat to people
So why threaten it?

Amir Gyunduz (10)

A Day In The Life Of A Greenhouse

G ardeners growing more green by the day, whilst everyone around me starts to play
R ivers streaming up and down, everywhere and all around
E merald so bright that it looks like the sun shining
E ach day children play until the night falls and when the day comes back again they wait for the rooster's morning call.
N ear me, the wind flows and blows, but never goes
H appily, the people dance and sing while wearing gorgeous-looking rings
O bstinate children standing their guard, being confident about whatever they're singing
U rgently people needing food, so they come to me for some herbs
S nowy days when people make snowmen and play
E xtraordinarily green inside, some big, some small, but to me, they're all very special.

Linah Elhag (10)
St Cuthbert's RC Primary School, Cardiff Bay

Queen Elizabeth II's Daily Life

Q uiet day today, sipping my tea in my fancy and fabulous castle
U nique day sitting in peace and harmony, watching the delightful view
E very day I go out and see my loving, wonderful people
E xcitedly, I went inside my royal castle and ate my delicious, masterpiece breakfast
N ow I will play with my adorable, cute corgis

E nergetically, I would read my interesting books, and sit and relax in my royal room (having a great time)
L ovely, I will look at my beautiful, pretty, colourful flowers in my garden
I happily go to have my amazing, fantastic walk
Z ooming, I went to have my fancy, appetising lunch
A ll the people I met were showing love, generosity and trust

- **B** eautifully, I had a good tea and ate in a peaceful time
- **E** very soldier was very helpful and they gave me beautiful flowers, they looked colourful and bright
- **T** oday was very fun and fantastic, today was my favourite
- **H** aving a good bedtime and waking up tomorrow.

Sara Orozgani
St Cuthbert's RC Primary School, Cardiff Bay

The Life Of A Stray

On a normal day still being a stray, not sure what to eat,
I'm totally beat, had no sleep last night, and didn't sleep till light
Coming home to my cardboard box, my only friend, a trash fox looking around
Some food I found, this will have to do,
I can't call a crew, and nobody here with me
Finding someone is just a myth
I'm fatigued, I suddenly became intrigued
By a piece of chicken on the ground that's just around the corner.
Came right to it, the taste was all right.
Days and nights I kept going, but still, I wasn't home,
Started to worry until I made it, I was kind of cold
The adventure was what I sought until I heard a tiny squeal, a tiny mouse,
But what I really wanted was a great big house
The mouse was still there, I grabbed it by a hair,
I was about to chomp, but I saw a chunk of perfectly good bread

I should take it as I don't have a bed
I ate it all up, then got chased by a pup
This is what it's like to be a stray
You might want to stay away.

Martha Devereux (9)
St Cuthbert's RC Primary School, Cardiff Bay

A Day Of A Diamond

A iming at the sun to make a shining, glowing effect

D rawing with water to make glossy drips
A mazingly shaped with the best edges
Y ellow sunflowers all around with people gazing into it

O ften, people never stop staring at it
F lowing wind blowing all the flowers into it

A quarium animals can't stop looking in shock

D ays make the diamond better not worse
I llustrators can't even illustrate that because it's so unique
A ll day, everyone wants to steal it
M arvellous sparkles bouncing off it
O range and yellow glitter
N ice and pretty sparkling colour
D ying to be bought by someone.

Leo John Tylke (9)
St Cuthbert's RC Primary School, Cardiff Bay

The Scary Monster

S cattering underground where sometimes you can't see under your bed
C rawling up your walls in the night getting ready to jump out
A rching over to see you at night in the dark
R eaching to catch you off guard in the day
Y ou will be terrified if you see it

M onsters love talking to kids, also animals
O bviously, you can't see it, it's always hiding
N ever try to find it because you will regret it
S ometimes it can be friendly
T he terrifying beast under your bed
E verything scary about the monster
w **R** ecking your bedroom when you're gone.

Blake Parris
St Cuthbert's RC Primary School, Cardiff Bay

How Messi's Day Goes

L iving a good life with friends and family
I love playing football, my fans were cheering
O verhearing my children cheering, my heart moved
N ow I left the football team, it was horrible
E ver since the football team, I practised more tricks
L ater I ate dinner with my family... delicious

M y kids get shy sometimes so I help them
E very day I go to work, they pay me a lot of money
S ometimes I take my family to the beach
S erious things are happening in the news about me
I miss playing football, maybe one day I will come back, I hope.

God'sthrone Davids (9)
St Cuthbert's RC Primary School, Cardiff Bay

Life Of A Smart And Speedy Greyhound

G rand prize, throwing sticks and having lots of licks
R ight, good time, nobody knows, so I got to bark
E xciting new walks and adventure willing for more
Y ou humans always petting me with amazed looks on your face
H ow I really want a treat, it makes me happy and a smile on your face
O bedient, I help in the kitchen with a smile on your face
U nique hugs from my friends and family I have all day
N ervous about spooky things and people shouting
D ependent, gets more food, helps and takes me for walks.

Isis Urzedo Zucolli
St Cuthbert's RC Primary School, Cardiff Bay

Sunny Flower POV

S izeable, immaculate sky with wind considerately flowing across the vivid grass
U nabashed, I gracefully swayed with the music playing
N aive and childish, I watched the children dancing and decided to join in
F lying in the sky, I saw a large plane
L onely, I sat there with no one to comfort me
O n my own, I wondered about the future, with no one to share it with
W et, it slowly started to rain
E xtraordinary plants surround me
R aindrops stroking my radiant petals.

Amara Elgabar (10)
St Cuthbert's RC Primary School, Cardiff Bay

Under The Sea

D olphins gracefully swimming through the calm, colourful coral
O ver the rocks as we swim happily as a pack and go for a snack
L ooking at the fresh coral as it shines and glimmers, our eyes alight
P ulling my friends along as we jump and dance and prance
H igh in the sky feeling as if I could fly, I never want it to end
I f I go out alone, I am always being watched
N ow that I've grown, I'm all alone, but I'm still a happy mammal.

Nailah Ellis (10)
St Cuthbert's RC Primary School, Cardiff Bay

Deep Blue Sea

M ighty mermaid swimming in the sea, living life, strong to be
E very scale you have shining through the sea, making you glow
R esting on the rock, breathing air, your hair blowing bright and polite
M agical face glaring at the coral
A ddictive eyes you look at all day, stare at them without looking away
I t always seems like you're fake, it's so hard to believe it
D oll face, big blue eyes, brown hair, way too nice.

Inayah Carpin (10)
St Cuthbert's RC Primary School, Cardiff Bay

The Terrific Turtle

T hrough the deep blue sea, I desperately look for food
U nable to hide from the spine-chilling, killing predators
R acing through the blue sea, sprinting like a turbo turtle
T ogether, the turtle and his friends depend on eating food
L ovely sight of the big blue sea, the turtle saw in awe
E agerly the turtle swam, enjoying the view of the sky so very blue.

Genelia Sharif (10)
St Cuthbert's RC Primary School, Cardiff Bay

A Doctor's Day

D oing my job as doctors always do
O h, and helping my wonderful patients feel better
C asting my beautiful patients so they can feel better
T rying my best to be a wonderful and kind doctor
O h everyone is thanking me and appreciating me, it just feels so nice
R ound and round the world and days go, being a wonderful and kind doctor.

Falak Navabjan
St Cuthbert's RC Primary School, Cardiff Bay

Blue Whale

B lue whales are bigger than my house
L ots of fish in their tummy
U nder the deep blue sea
E xcited to see one when I go swimming

W hales are beautiful and kind
H ow noble and cute small blue whale
A blue whale is kind
L ovely smooth blue skin
E ven be seen from the sky.

Anas Albalawi
St Cuthbert's RC Primary School, Cardiff Bay

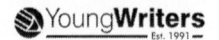

The Crown

T he Queen helps poor people
H er beautiful crown on her head
E xcitement on the street

Q ueen of the world
U nderstanding how to laugh
E xcited to see her corgis
E xcited to do our tour
N ow she is with Philip again.

Rayanna Abyan
St Cuthbert's RC Primary School, Cardiff Bay

Sunflower

S unflower so much sun down its stem
U nderground the roots do flow
N ow on the petals there was a water droplet
F un and friendly
L ots of friends
O range and yellow
W et and gloomy
E asy life
R ed and green.

Suhaib Hassan (10)
St Cuthbert's RC Primary School, Cardiff Bay

The Life Of A Tree Throughout The Seasons

Spring is here
Time to seed all the flowers
Sway in the breeze
The blossom as pink as bubblegum
The aroma as sweet as marshmallows
Summer is here
The sun is a skin burner in the sky
There are ripples of oak going down my spine
The sun can turn your skin the colour crimson
I feel warm inside like you are my sun
Autumn is here
Canary orange leaves, hazelnut-coloured leaves
The wind whistles as it runs through the leaves like fingers
There are apples full with juicy ripeness
Winter is here
You wrap up all nice and warm, the snow like porcelain.

Ellie Grainger (10)
St George's Primary School, Church Gresley

Our Trees Are Beautiful

N ever forget the summer, it will come back
A utumn is cold for me because I lose my leaves
T rees are important, they give you air
U s trees are used to the warmth
R espect us, we give you air
E xcellent trees are always around.

I ce cream is cold
S uper summer shall be around once every year

O ut in nature all of the time
U nknown things are always on trees
R est in the sweltering heat
S uper summer makes me burn.

Reuben Marshall (10)
St George's Primary School, Church Gresley

Super Seasons

S ummer is a delightfully hot time, but I can provide you with shade
E ven though leaves fall off me in autumn, I get to see children laugh and play in the leaves
A utumn leaves, orange, red and yellow fall off me as fruit grows on my lovely branches
S pring is my favourite as marshmallow pink and daisy white blossom grows onto me and keeps me warm
O n a warm summer day, my branches bathe in the flower-growing sun
N ow so cold and crisp, the snow falls around me and my leaves leave me again.

Ethan Colley (10)
St George's Primary School, Church Gresley

Santa Claus

S nowy days are back
A ll of the fascinating lights
N ight of my reindeer taking flight
T ime flies by when you're having fun
A lthough, no more sun

C old days, but always amazed
L ove at home with family and friends
A lways making children happy
U nder the world, but always making presents
S anta buys presents while people are eating presents (for Christmas dinner) and that's Christmas.

Abigail Hawksworth (10)
St George's Primary School, Church Gresley

Help

I'm hurt, I'm being destroyed
Why do you hate me?
My trees are being cut down
My ocean has been polluted
My animals have been killed
Someone help me
My air is filled with gas
My streets, my towns, my cities are covered in litter
Help!
People are hurting my air with cigarettes
They're hurting my forests
They're hurting my creations
They're hurting me
Stop! Help me! Before it's too late.

Charlotte Roden (10)
St George's Primary School, Church Gresley

The War

Day four of being in the war
I don't know what to do because it's spreading even more
There's a hurricane that's getting even bigger
It might suck me up, as well as Mary and Trever
If you didn't know, Trever is my brother and also
The same saviour of my mother
Uh, now it's time to duck as the hurricane is going berserk.
Finally, it's over, the cotton-like cloud put out the fire.

Harrison Poulton (10)
St George's Primary School, Church Gresley

All The Things I Can See

O ngoing boats riding beyond me, on my smooth body
C olossal whales diving into me ever so carefully
E legant fish swarming around and blowing perfectly circular bubbles
A stonishing sharks with their white and glowing teeth, regularly get troubles
N ever-ending sizzling surf calming my tide down with its calming sound.

Isla Wilson (10)
St George's Primary School, Church Gresley

The Seasonal Cloud

As I block out the sun
I stop people
From having some sun
Whilst I sit in the skies
The sad tears
Flutter from my eyes
When they wet the people below
It shows me that they like it more when it snows
When it hails
I hear their wails
But when I move away
They come back out to play.

William Hadley (10)
St George's Primary School, Church Gresley

Nature Is Amazing

N ature is beautiful
A utumn is cold for me because I start to lose my leaves
T rees are good because we give you air
U s trees need to be protected
R espect us trees, we are precious
E lder trees are at risk of getting sick.

Ava Mcclenahan (11)
St George's Primary School, Church Gresley

Chester's Life

C all me Chester
H arry is my bro
E ven my ears are cute
S is calls them a fluffy blanket
T raitor, my mum groomed an impostor
E ven though I'm her favourite
R ats are like cats, as they both annoy me.

Harry Topliss (10)
St George's Primary School, Church Gresley

The Life Of A Door

D oorbell, ring me to let people know that you are there
O pen me, close me, whatever you would like
O verseeing who is really there, making sure they don't give you a scare
R ight at the front of the house, being shown to the world!

Orla-Lily Edwards (10)
St George's Primary School, Church Gresley

The Earth's Riddle

You live on me
Such a beautiful place to be
The green grass
The blue sky
A mysterious ocean
And wonderful animals to have
Cute ones, scary ones
Good ones, bad ones
Who am I?

Answer: I'm Planet Earth.

Zack Gee (10)
St George's Primary School, Church Gresley

Grasslands

N ow I stand in front of my friends
A nd we stand there waiting
T he things came to us
U nknown things chop down the trees
"R etreat, retreat!" I shout
E vil comes as we find a new home.

Amarla-Rose Armstrong (10)
St George's Primary School, Church Gresley

The Four Seasons

T he summer brings a sweltering sun that
R etracts into autumn where the leaves retreat for the winter
E ntering winter, the snowy days begin to retreat into spring
E ntering spring, the blossom explodes with joy.

Ben Sparshott (10)
St George's Primary School, Church Gresley

Famous Footballer Lionel Messi's Poem

I'm about to score a goal
But I missed it
Went again and got a goal
I'm dribbling and I'm good
I got tackled but I got it back and I tripped
I got it back
I told my friend and team that I got a goal.

Kayden Murdoch (11)
St George's Primary School, Church Gresley

Tree Goes On And On

T he trees look like a freshly-picked broccoli
R ight to left trees look beautiful
E very season trees change like food rotting
E ven when it rains trees will go up to the moon like a beanstalk.

Jonah Hallam (10)
St George's Primary School, Church Gresley

Mystery

I swing side to side
I cling to things
I soar through the sky
I was bit by a spider
I have a red and blue suit.
Who am I?

Answer: *Spider-Man*.

Joe Haywood (10)
St George's Primary School, Church Gresley

The Mystery

I can see and walk
But never seem to talk
The sunlight, amazing
Makes me too dizzy
I can fly so
What am I?

Answer: I'm an angel!

Phoebe Rand (10)
St George's Primary School, Church Gresley

The Trees

T oday I have been fed
R oots help me grow
E agles land on me
E agles know I am not a landing spot
S un shines on me.

Alfie Haywood (10)
St George's Primary School, Church Gresley

What A Tree Can See Throughout The Year

T errific winter came
R aining spring was not the same
E xcellent summer was a good aim
E xcept autumn was an amazing gain.

Riley Ross (10)
St George's Primary School, Church Gresley

The Happy Tree

T all tree stands high
R ed sky is soothing
E very kid comes past, and says "Hi!"
E nd of the story.

Niamh Flynn (10)
St George's Primary School, Church Gresley

What The Moon Knows

The moon
The secrets I know
The marvellous wonders
A wise watcher of the dark night
The moon.

Olivia Evans (11)
St George's Primary School, Church Gresley

The Big Monkey

T he big, jumping monkey loves to play
H e is always doing something fun
E ven though he has lots of fun, he is still sometimes angry, it's hard work being a big monkey!

B ehold, the big monkey has many friends, they love to play in the sun
I n the monkey's heart, he is lovely and kind and always has tons of fun
"G o, go!" said one of the monkey's friends, faster!

M aybe the monkey is a little too fun sometimes
O n Sundays, it doesn't even have breakfast
N obody can stop it from having fun
K itty is the monkey's best friend, they have been best friends since they were one
E very day they have such spontaneous fun
"Y um, yum! Bananas are my favourite snack," says the monkey.

Leonida-Lilly Saez Mortimer (9)
St Joseph's Catholic Primary School, Northfleet

Me And My Swim

And there I stood, by the side of the pool
Looking down at the water, my reflection staring back at me
Taking a deep breath, goggles on, preparing for my lesson
"I can do this!" stepping with each foot
Onto the steps
Glistening water soaked me as I positioned myself to swim
A shot of adrenaline ran through my body
And I started to kick my legs
Holding my breath, I gazed at the water
It was calm, my calm place
Then, as I looked up, there was splashing
And noise
I felt proud
I had made it to the other side, and what fun it was!
'My experience, my swim.'

Flavia Mazzocca (8)
St Joseph's Catholic Primary School, Northfleet

Gabriel Jesus

G reat Gaby does a lot for us
A rsenal love the lad when he scores for us
B est boy in the land
R ed kits (Arsenal kits) suit the lad
I n the Emirates is his home
E ventually, he will be as good as Pelé
L ucky, lucky Arsenal to have such a good player

J olly, jolly Gabriel Jesus
E xtraordinary player in my opinion
S uper with the ball at his feet
U nbelievable experience to watch him play
S ilent when not playing football, but extremely loud while playing.

Freddy Lawlor (8)
St Joseph's Catholic Primary School, Northfleet

Friends Are Important

F riendship matters since you don't want to be lonely, do you?
R elationships with people you don't know aren't great because you can't trust them
I ll-treating people is just one way to lose friends
E nding friendships is okay if you can't get along with them very well
N ot playing with someone regularly doesn't mean you aren't friends
D ifferences between your friends (skin colour, eye colour etc.) don't mean you can't be friends!
S haring is caring!

Temilayo Adesina (8)
St Joseph's Catholic Primary School, Northfleet

My Cat

My cat is as frail as an autumn leaf
But her purr is as loud as the seas
Her claws are as gnarled as an ancient oak
And she'll always belong to me.

Her fur is as soft as a kitten's coat
But her eyes are as soft as the breeze
Her eyes are as black as the blackest pearl
And she'll always belong to me.

She sits by the fire and tries to keep warm
Or she curls herself up on my knees
Her dreams are as light as a feathered leap
But her memory belongs to me.

Michael Ayenuro (10)
St Joseph's Catholic Primary School, Northfleet

A Doggy Day

Digging in the mud
Messy like a pig
Wagging its little tail
It's a doggy day

Having some fun with his spotty friend
Barking and playing like the day will never end
Wearing a party hat
Getting tired
Lying down
It's a doggy day.

Running in for water
Holding their breath
Muddy footprints
On the checkered floor
It's a doggy day.

Alya Shah (8)
St Joseph's Catholic Primary School, Northfleet

A Trip Around Space

A trip around space never ended
A trip around space was glory
It was miles long and I wanted more
A trip around space lasted years
A trip around space was delightful
Go back I might
A trip around space I enjoyed
A trip around space, I needed to go, I pleaded
I had a good time, I know I went to space
I'll live a good life, not being a disgrace.

Ite Jolaoso (10)
St Joseph's Catholic Primary School, Northfleet

Flying

F lying looks fun, I wish I could try
L ook at their amazing wings, soaring into the sky
Y ou are the best, most beautiful butterfly I have ever seen
I n-flight with your friends like a colourful team
N ever staying still, always beating your wings
G oing from place to place, how much joy you bring.

Connie Oxtoby (8)
St Joseph's Catholic Primary School, Northfleet

Arsenal

A rsenal is my favourite club in football history
R ivals are Spurs
S o skilful and attacking
E xcellent football team
N ever loses a match
A rsenal is the best team in the world
L osing a match is something we don't do.

Enyinna Okolie (8)
St Joseph's Catholic Primary School, Northfleet

Summer

S ummertime is a time for flowers and blossom
U nusually hot and humid weather
M y favourite season has passed by
M ay is the month to go to the beach
E veryone covered in sweat from head to toe
R eady for the cold to start.

Kyra Manan (9)
St Joseph's Catholic Primary School, Northfleet

Our Queen

It's hard to see you fall
But England is standing tall
You are now a recurring bird
I cried when I heard
You have left history
But we are sad to see your children grieve
Rest in peace with Philip
You will forever be our Queen.

Hannah Mahon (10)
St Joseph's Catholic Primary School, Northfleet

The Why Of The Coyote

Why, world, why?
You saw my family die
So do this for me, please
Bring them back for me
Why, Sun, why?
Did you have to be at your brightest yesterday?
I really didn't like it, 40 degrees C, I had no water
I felt like I was burning away
It wasn't a very nice day
Seeing my family go
My dreams shattered
I could taste the burnt bodies in the air
Rain fell and lightning clattered
Dear world, dear sun, dear humans
Why don't you show empathy for mothers?
Think about it
If your family died would you be happy about it?
No.
You all look upon me as a coyote with no feelings
Well, I do have feelings.

Aaliyah Oluseye (10)
Stroud Green Primary School, London

Humans And The Amazon

Hello, I'm the Amazon
I am getting smaller by the day thanks to you
Humans cutting my trees
Fleeing animals running at the scene
Humans have stolen their homes
Disobeying nature's command only for their gain
One day, I hope one of you will rise
I'm worth fighting for
Alas, I don't know
I hear Ocean is having the same problem
Plastic swimming in his ocean
Strangling fish left and right
Until there are no more in sight
And finally air
Slowly suffocating-no one cares
Birds being poisoned by CO_2
You need to make a stand
Or there might not be a tomorrow
Future or now.

Nate Gosling (10)
Stroud Green Primary School, London

Save Our Branches

I know you can do that, you can help us
Get a plant in your hand, make a tiny tree grow up
Be friends with the world, change the world
If you can do it, everyone will think of us.
The books made from my family
We might die, we can't know that
My dream was to live with my family
But now I can't, they killed my family
Have empathy for me
Is your family that good? No!
You think I'm just a tree
I don't have feelings, but I do.

Nilay Dogruoglu (11)
Stroud Green Primary School, London

Life Of A Fish

Every day my brothers and sisters
Get taken away and it's only peaceful
When predators wait till day
Who knows, I might be next
But now I know everyone is trying their best
I am hunting for food, looking for prey
And I don't know if I'll die today
I try to survive day and night
But only then do the predators fight
Day and night the seaweeds sway
From side to side
The predators will find me so I
Need to hide.

Fernando Goncalves Miguel (10)
Stroud Green Primary School, London

The Snake

I live in the rainforest and the trees are getting cut down
I have nowhere to live
I pounce at my predators and then I attack
I am not scared of anything except for the man in the red van
I can slither anywhere, that is how I escape
I hiss and everyone runs away
I am not endangered, although I think I might get extinct
Every day it's cold
When the man with the red van comes
I feel so much wind from the animal stampede.

Mouna Ahouddar (10)
Stroud Green Primary School, London

My Younger Brother

When I see younger kids
It reminds me of when I was young
If only those days would come back
It would be a dream come true
I start to do more and more
Since I want to be an example
For my younger brother
I hope he will be just like me
When he will be my age
I want to take care of Earth
I want to be an example
For my brother and more people
I hope they will do
What I do.

Alessandro Boghean (10)
Stroud Green Primary School, London

Save Us

These may be my last words:

S onic-speed bullets piercing through my skin
A nimals are sprinting away from the loud bangs
V ampire-like bats are crying and flying for their life
E lephants are stomping their giant feet in fright

U nder the tree, I can see a man holding an axe
S o please, oh please, save us!

Zinedine Laifa (10)
Stroud Green Primary School, London

Lion Call

Soon I'll have nowhere to go
My stomach rumbles like thunder
Waiting for my next meal
The grass tickles my body as I crouch down low
I hear a crash, a tree fell down
Scaring away my prey
My family is disappearing
Now it's only me
My forest and my kind are getting killed
For I'm an Asiatic lion
And this is my call.

Suzie Parker (10)
Stroud Green Primary School, London

Daylight

D arkness
A nd no light to be seen
Y onder is nowhere, no left, no right, or straight
L ove was never here, no such word as love
I wonder why I'm here, just floating
G loom surrounds us everywhere
H ateful words echo around this 'home'
T hree minutes left, I have no choice.

Darla Thomas-Thompson (10)
Stroud Green Primary School, London

The Ocean Master

My master is endless, all-powerful
Constantly, he churns up matter, refining it, grounding it, polishing it
He is the giver of life, master of death
He gives homes, nourishment, great opportunities
My master is joy, sadness, hope
He rules the water, obeyed by all
He is inevitable
The ocean master.

Laurence Lachmann (10)
Stroud Green Primary School, London

Squirrel's Life Cycle

I am a squirrel, as sneaky as can be
I hope you've got some ice for your knees
Because this poem is like a comedy
I live in a tall tree
Every spring I collect nuts
Why? For winter
Please tell me what is a splinter.

Xianna Rose-Locke (8)
Stroud Green Primary School, London

A Baby Orangutan

I could see a golden glaze on a mango
I could hear trees getting cut down low
I could smell the wet mud
Where I had dug
I tasted a banana that was delicious
I touched a tree with missing bark, which was suspicious.

Yanaëlle B (8)
Stroud Green Primary School, London

Look Outside

F ast-blowing wind
L ucious green leaves
O range leaves
W ish I was outside
E legant birds
R ustling leaves.

Iris Mcananey (8)
Stroud Green Primary School, London

I Am The Ocean Baby

I am an ocean baby
I live in the ocean, all the plastic swims around me
Every day I yearn for clean, clear water
All I want is clean, crystal-clear water.

Hayaat Mohamed (10)
Stroud Green Primary School, London

Laughing As We Die

Peace, serenity, happiness
Until they invaded and ruined us, our community
Weapons, axes, shouting, axes
Smiling as they hurt us
Laughing as we die.

Rosa Niland (10)
Stroud Green Primary School, London

Monkey

I live in the trees
I scavenge in the jungle
I watch my brothers die
Trees come and go
I don't know if this will be my last day.

Miska Barton (10)
Stroud Green Primary School, London

The Bird
A haiku

A bird in its cage
For I am that tiny bird
When will I be free?

Zoe Katona (10)
Stroud Green Primary School, London

Life Of A Dog

Some people think I'm special
Some think I'm a burden
I walk the streets with my owner and get attention
Some think I'm special, some think I'm a burden
I do tricks for treats
At Easter, I'm a bunny
Halloween right around the corner
I chase squirrels
My owner says "Naughty boy!"
I whine and whimper
I go for a walk
I know I'm special, not a burden
I'm kind to the nice, bark at the bad
Some think I'm special, some think I'm a burden.

Chloe Parker (10)
The Sir Donald Bailey Academy, Newark

I See More

I eat and eat
Until I can't anymore
I have many feet
I love to crawl
Then after a while
I'll lie in a heap
On a leaf
Under the moon
I won't move for a while
Because I'm starting a cocoon
You'll see me soar
After I've spread my wings
I'll see more.

Amelia Needham (10)
The Sir Donald Bailey Academy, Newark

Goodbye Queen Elizabeth 2022

You reigned for seventy years
We are all in tears
Please come back
We need you
We all loved you
You were the best
Goodbye Queen Elizabeth

I wish I had met you
But I never got the chance
I loved seeing you on the telly
Now I can't...
When the bells ring
It reminds me of you
Goodbye Queen Elizabeth

When the town's asleep in bed
The bells ring
Ring for Queen Elizabeth

Over and over again
Goodbye Queen Elizabeth!

Isabella Hudson (10)
The Sir Donald Bailey Academy, Newark

Queen Elizabeth

I found you, tell me to do stuff
I sat making rules
But did you follow them?
I was brave, I always had to smile
It's now King Charles III's time
As I lie dead while England stays in peace
I'm buried with Prince Philip
Did you care?
Now I will lie in my coffin.

Ashley Muller (10)
The Sir Donald Bailey Academy, Newark

Lightning Strikes
A haiku

Piercing the night sky
I look for objects to strike
My thunder growling.

Paige Keetley (10)
The Sir Donald Bailey Academy, Newark

An Evacuee's Story

Boom! Bombs dropping around me
Mum's petrified pale face rung in my mind as
We huddled up in the tin can shelter
As a cloud of smoke snaked around me
Me and my sister were taken to some unknown, hustling and bustling place

With choking tags
We coughed like hags, losing our way
We'd rather play
Waving goodbye was like drowning in tears
As the train screeched like a parrot with a cough
Put into lines one by one
Losing siblings put with strangers
Who knows who's the danger?

We were put into a hall
Thankfully, with my sister beside me
Strangers walked past us, pointing and picking
Then when someone headed our way, I began to pray
That they would choose both of us

"I pick you two," she said.

Giggling and playing, doing rock, paper, scissors,
This is a different scene to Hull
Instead of the murky unknown territory above us
It was a territory I hadn't seen for years!

As we drew up to the picturesque cottage
She opened the door and we decided
We'll write to Mum
Up we went, one by one
Unpacking our stuff, we wrote a letter

Dear Mum,
Vita in hoc novo loco bene est...interesting.
Little Ann has settled in great and I really miss you!
And if you do have any news from Dad, please tell us.

Lots of love from,

Lola and Ann
xxx

Amelie Scott (10)
Wold Newton Foundation School, Wold Newton

The Unseen War

Like an ear-piercing siren
The screams of my friends sound like a roaring lion
Bent double like old beggars under sacks
We never have any time to relax
Knock-kneed, coughing like hags
Never again I'd be a normal lad

Every day saying bye to my friends
Sometimes I think to myself
Is this nightmare ever gonna end?
The feeling of this one week feels very long
Hoping I'll be there to write the next one

The wind howled in the night
Most stay awake because of their fright
Seeing the Germans ready with their guns
Then I realised there was no more time for fun

All of a sudden, something frightening happened
"Gas, gas, gas, quick!" shouted someone
"Quick, quick, quick!" screamed another
"Help, my gas mask won't go on!"
He died a slow painful death

As we chucked his body in the pile, row on row
I heard someone say my bullet supply was very low
But before I could ever answer he lost his battle
Eyes as white as a ghost
Now he's a part of their host

As I gripped my gun
My mouth as dry as a desert
I took my first gunshot
Boom!
Sicut in me iaculis glande desperatum sciebam me.

Georgia Emmerson (10)
Wold Newton Foundation School, Wold Newton

The Soldier

A true soldier doesn't fight
Because of what's in front of him
He fights because he loves
What's behind him

Soldiers begging for the war
To be over and finished
Soldiers begging for a
Good night's sleep

Soldiers wondering if they
Will see their families again
Soldiers wondering if they
Will be able to hear again
After the bombs and gunshots
Had deafened them

Bombs, bullets and grenades
Going off every minute
Soldiers trying to dodge them

When night falls, fighting
Doesn't stop

Blood-curdling into the ground
All I could smell were rotting bodies
Soldiers gagging and floundering
When getting gassed
Soldiers fumbling, trying to get their masks on

All the soldiers trying
To climb up the trenches
Trying to escape the gas
Soldiers falling back into the gas

Boom! Bang!
Blood leaking out of the soldiers' bodies
Soldiers dying due to climbing
Out of the soggy, muddy trenches.

Joseph Newton (11)
Wold Newton Foundation School, Wold Newton

Finally Picked

My brother, my brother
I cried out loud
I've lost him, I've lost him
He's been picked
Please, oh, please
Will someone take me
Finally, thank you, thank you
Floundering about with my gas mask

I'm questioning myself
Who is this woman?
Is she friendly or not?

I remember on the train
I had my head in my hands, sobbing
At least half the way
The further away from the station we got
The harder it was to hear the Bosche bombs
Although it was upsetting, it was magnificent
I've never seen views so incredible

Every day I look up and say
Dad, please don't die, please don't

In my bed, at night, I hear the wind howl
I think, how would that be for him?

My mum, now a Canary Girl
Does she still remember me?
Has she been killed?
She doesn't send me letters anymore
Who knows, who knows?

Ebony Warters (10)
Wold Newton Foundation School, Wold Newton

For All I Knew

For all I knew
It wasn't all glory
This moment has stained my baffled mind
My time-healed eyes will tell a loathsome story

The thick, sodden walls that surrounded me
A long, narrow shelter made to protect me
A riot of soldiers with lice-infected sores barging past me
My beloved children were sent away without me
An explosive thud echoed behind me.

An ecstasy of leaking gas surrounded me like a green sea
I was fumbling for my mask
Trembling with fear
I glanced behind me, a body was near

Helpless wails that break the air
His burnt throat corrupted
His weathered eyes bulged like squids

Taken under one's wing, a part of a team
An urge for help
"Medic! Medic! Man down!"
I scream

You may think the war was a victory story
Though, like I first said, it wasn't all glory.

Ellie Davison (11)
Wold Newton Foundation School, Wold Newton

Canariae Puellae

This job gets hazardous
This is what I do though,
I have done this before
In World War I
So I can do this
I remember what to do
My hands are turning yellow
I guess that's why people call me a 'Canary Girl'
The burning smell of oil
I'm soon going to taste it
It hasn't gotten any better
The guttering is the machine
I hope it doesn't fall on me
These bombs feel like Antarctica
They are so gravis
I hope my children are okay.
Bombs, bullets, making them row by row
Don't drop it, don't drop it,
Or else it will blow
I need to stay determined
Like I did for World War I

I was only twenty-two
I'm doing everything I can
Nos semper concurias.

Rose Harrison (10)
Wold Newton Foundation School, Wold Newton

Evacuee

On a train from Hell, I'm terrified
Where it's super dull, the train was rusty
I waved bye to Mother with dread
As the train speeds up
Away I go, I miss my family
Children everywhere, I get lost
I gather my things, ready to go
I arrived at the house
Swirls of smoke from the chimney
I hope I'll see my family soon
I hope they're kind like they promised
The village is better than I thought
I glanced at them, they didn't notice
The wind howled as I looked out
I went to see Mother and Father again.
It's been a month
"Can I go home now?"
"Can I go home now?"
"Can I go home?"
Now a month feels like a year
I want to see my family again.

Dallas Kirman (9)
Wold Newton Foundation School, Wold Newton

The Tank

I detected the trees trembling in front of me
As I rolled up to a Jerry tank
My body went cold
I took a deep breath
And realised that my country is in my small hands

Whilst opening the rusty hatch
I was clutching my hands onto the cold, metal grenade
Bang! A gas bomb hit the battlefield, surrounding me
My hand was shaking, trying to fit my gas mask on
My ally drowning in a green sea of gas
While his throat burnt in agony
His withering body leapt at me as
He clutched onto my jacket helplessly
I've been here for years, fighting for my country
With a sparkle of hope
But my hope crumbles
As this war, in my eyes, is never-ending.

Lorence Blyth (10)
Wold Newton Foundation School, Wold Newton

Evacuee

I never wanted this day to come
World War II has come
This is not gonna be fun
Evacuated on a train
Praying to God our families will be safe
My heart started to crumble into pieces
Mother said bye
Brother said bye
Mother began to cry
I trembled whilst
Getting on the train
I trembled whilst being taken to a hall
I was confused to have a new home
I was second in line
I was taken
Why me?
Why me?
I can't live without my family
What if they die?
I slept until morning rise
I sent Mum a letter asking if she was okay

I was worried sick
I wanted to go back
She said no, you can't come home, not yet
Hopefully soon.
A few months have passed.

Laycie Rutherford (11)
Wold Newton Foundation School, Wold Newton

Me The Evacuee

As I pack my suitcase
To say goodbye
I will miss you, Mum
I will miss you, Dad
Bye, bye!
I am on the train
I wave with a brave face
But then I burst into tears
Watching bombs go low, *boom!*
Bullets fly by
And planes fly high
I am terrified
I clutch my suitcase
And gas mask
While going by
When I got off the train
I didn't know where to go
I was terrified
Can I come home now?
I have been here for years
I arrived at a hall with thousands of children

Overwhelmed with tears
Can I come home now?
I have been here for years
Please, please, please
Uneasy
Yes, you can come home now
The war has gone.

Emma-Jo Wheeler (9)
Wold Newton Foundation School, Wold Newton

Evacuee Life

I am an evacuee
It's a dreadful experience
Like a marching soldier, I was forced onto the train
Feeling like I was going to sob
Now leaving all this at last
Forgetting what I've seen in the past
Now I've arrived at the village
I'm really hoping someone accepts my image
My family is gone
Feeling abandoned, and missing them all
My mother no longer tucks me in at night
It was always a delight
My father told me scary stories
But sadly, they've come true
I can't wait for it to return to me and you
I wrote a letter to Father
But Mother replied
Saying he has gone
I didn't even get time to say goodbye.

Lily Yeadon (10)
Wold Newton Foundation School, Wold Newton

Canariae Puellae

It's happened again, another war
Every morning, day on day
I hate putting on these clothes
Guttering is the machine
I hope it doesn't fall on me

Bombs, bullets, making them row on row
Don't drop it, don't drop it or else it will blow
The feel of the bombs is like a checkered board
Seeing the bombs and the bullets off in the truck
It feels like the weight has been lifted, not for long

My arms are covered in gunpowder
Yes, I may die from it
And my children would be wounded badly
But it's good to die for your loving country
No semper Canariae Puellae.

Emily Garrick
Wold Newton Foundation School, Wold Newton

The Dambuster

As I soar so high
Through the murky sky
I observe the enemy
Surrounding the soldiers
That are gagging
As the poisonous green gas
Drives them to Heaven

As I fly to Germany
A Jerry plan is spotted
We try to lose it but we can't
We fire our military cannons
Blowing them up out of the sky
They are going down, down
Down into the river

We are getting closer to Germany
We can hear whizz-bangs in the distance
Bang, crash! We have hit the dam
Flooding the town
The Germans have spotted us

We fly out of there
Dam destroyed, I radio
Base perfecta missione.

Toby Pinder (11)
Wold Newton Foundation School, Wold Newton

World War II At Sea

Here we are with HMS Belfast.
Clearing a way for a convoy of a hundred ships.
We have our worst enemy, Admiral Grafspee.
We have ten American destroyers with us.
We have HMS Ark Royal with us.
I live on HMS Hood.
My job before was as a mechanic,
Now I am a ship mechanic
The engine roars like a thunderstorm.
What do you think the engine sounds like?
We all wait for the call.
"Abandon ship! Abandon ship!"
I heard that call, I didn't think I would ever hear that call.

Charlie Emmerson (9)
Wold Newton Foundation School, Wold Newton

WWII: A Day In My Plane

In my plane flying through briefly, looking at clouds
With people getting gassed below me
They are fighting for their lives, fighting for their country
And for their family
We have arrived at Austria to try to help France
Because their country is getting powerfully affected
We have started fighting
Planes crashing, people shouting
People dying, planes bombing
People running and cities getting whizz-bangs.

William Traves (10)
Wold Newton Foundation School, Wold Newton

WWII

As I walk through the sludging mud
Tanks migrate like an earthquake
A grenade shot through the sky
Like a hawk, I soon realise this isn't good
"Quick, quick, gas boys!"
As I drown in the gas
I have a flashback of my family at home.

Lewis Kirk (10)
Wold Newton Foundation School, Wold Newton

Gas

Gas, Gas! As the green smoke
Rushed around us
We fumbled with our gas masks
The soldier didn't make it in time
His throat burning with agony
His eyes staring at me hopelessly.

Lailah Chandler (10)
Wold Newton Foundation School, Wold Newton

YOUNG WRITERS INFORMATION

We hope you have enjoyed reading this book – and that you will continue to in the coming years.

If you're the parent or family member of an enthusiastic poet or story writer, do visit our website **www.youngwriters.co.uk/subscribe** and sign up to receive news, competitions, writing challenges and tips, activities and much, much more! There's lots to keep budding writers motivated!

If you would like to order further copies of this book, or any of our other titles, then please give us a call or order via your online account.

Young Writers
Remus House
Coltsfoot Drive
Peterborough
PE2 9BF
(01733) 890066
info@youngwriters.co.uk

Join in the conversation!
Tips, news, giveaways and much more!

YoungWritersUK   YoungWritersCW   youngwriterscw